GW01326637

# UNDEFEATED

## "OLD IRONSIDES" IN THE WAR OF 1812

*Commander Tyrone G. Martin*
*U. S. Navy (Retired)*

*Illustrations by*
*John Charles Roach*
*U.S. Navy Combat Artist*

**A Timonier Book**

TRYON PUBLISHING COMPANY, INC.
CHAPEL HILL • TRYON

Copyright © 1996  Tyrone G. Martin
All rights reserved.  No part of this book may be reproduced
in any form or by any electronic, mechanical or other means,
except for brief quotes for reviews, without express written
permission from the publisher.

Printed in the United States of America
Published by
Tryon Publishing Company, Inc.
P.O. Box 1138
Chapel Hill, North Carolina

Cover & Book Design by Julia Calhoun Williams


*First Edition, Second Printing*

ISBN 1-884824-19-6

# TABLE OF CONTENTS

# INTRODUCTION

Early in 1794, the United States Congress was faced with the problem of assaults by the Barbary pirates of North Africa against American merchant ships in and near the Mediterranean Sea. As deliberations concerning this problem began, *Philadelphia* shipbuilder Joshua Humphreys wrote a letter to an influential political friend setting forth his ideas concerning the character of any newly authorized navy. He said that, since the young country could not afford many ships, those built should be designed to be stronger than any of their type and faster than any larger and stronger men-of-war. Humphreys was later selected to design the first units of the United States Navy, and his stated philosophy was basic to his plans.

The War of 1812 began with the Treaty of Paris of 1783 which granted independence to the United States of America. From the view of the British leadership, it was a paper forced upon them by the growing cost of putting down the rebellion and the increasing disaffection of the British people with the course of events. Deep down the British believed the colonies had not really been inalienably lost.

This attitude was soon made clear to the new nation. Ships bearing the American flag were not welcome to trade in British home or colonial ports except at a disadvantage. When attacked by Barbary pirates in the Mediterranean, there was no longer the long arm of the Royal Navy for protection. Thus, when revolutionary France overflowed its borders and embroiled Britain in a war that ultimately would last for decades, it was inevitable that the United States, with past links to both sides, would be caught in the middle.

Initially, in the mid to late 1790s, it was the French who irritated the Americans with the resulting Quasi-War with France. A developing United States Navy even cooperated with the Royal Navy to some extent in the West Indies. However, following the conclusion of that "un-war," and the subsequent collapse of the 1801 Peace of Amiens between France and Britain, Britain was pushed to extremes in efforts to defend herself against the Napoleonic juggernaut and to sustain the Royal Navy as her first line of defense. It was a bit of political pragmatism to adopt a course of "once an Englishman, always an Englishman" and impress Yankee seamen right out of their ships on the high seas so that British warships could have adequate crews. After all, prior to the American Revolution, these same colonies had provided about one-third of the men and ships comprising the British merchant marine.

During both his terms in office, President Thomas Jefferson unsuccessfully sought to deal with the situation by means short of war. With the advent of James Madison in the White House, the long-smoldering pressures for more direct action erupted. On 18 June 1812, the Congress declared war on Great Britain. Some felt this act long overdue, while many others were opposed because the conflict would ruin trade.

It was during this war that Joshua Humphreys' heavy frigate *Constitution* earned her nickname of "Old Ironsides" and became an icon of American sovereignty. At the war's declaration, *Constitution* was just completing a two-month overhaul at the Washington Navy Yard. In early July, she put to sea and had a close call when chased by a British squadron. By clever shiphandling, she escaped, and after a brief stop at Boston, began the voyages that attained for her immeasurable honor. In these pages are told the stories of the three battles that gained her a premier place in American history and proved, as no other ship has done, the correctness of her designer's concept.

*Tyrone G. Martin*

*Devil's Ridge*
*1 February 1996*

# UNDEFEATED

QUARTER DECK WATCH
OFFICERS AND MEN AT THEIR
STATIONS BY THE SHIP'S HELM IS THE SAILING MASTER, A
STAFF OFFICER, RESPONSIBLE FOR TAKING THE
SHIP WHEREVER THE CAPTAIN ORDERS. ON THE HIGH SIDE
OR WINDWARD THE SENIOR HELMSMAN WOULD STAND ASSISTED
BY ANOTHER MAN ON THE OTHER SIDE. THE COMPASSES ARE IN
TWO BINNACLES FORWARD OF THE SHIPS WHEEL.

# PART I

Connecticut Yankee Isaac Hull was no stranger to *Constitution*. He had served in her original wardroom as Fourth Lieutenant, and had risen to First Lieutenant under Commodore Silas Talbot before succeeding him in command when Talbot abruptly resigned in September 1801. Hull remained in caretaker command until February 1802. During the Barbary War, Hull first served as First Lieutenant of the frigate *Adams*, 28 guns, then commanded the schooner *Enterprize*, 12, and the brig *Argus*, 14. In these ships he served with increasing distinction. Indeed, his *Argus* was the principal naval support for the Arab-United States Marine assault on the Libyan city of Derne in 1805.

When he took command of *Constitution* in June 1810, Hull was thirty-seven years of age and had been a Captain for four years. A serious, thorough-going seaman, the short, rotund bachelor skipper was not as much concerned with the perquisites of rank as with the readiness of his command and the welfare of his crew.

. Captain Hull sailed from Boston on Sunday, 2 August 1812. He planned to attack British shipping around the entrance to the Gulf of St. Lawrence, expecting to wreak considerable damage on merchantmen as yet unaware of the war's outbreak. In the following

11

two weeks, he took a half dozen prizes, and then, sailing from Cape Race, decided to head for Bermudian waters, where he could possibly repeat such surprise attacks.

Hull steered in a generally southwesterly direction through out the 18th and 19th of August, occasionally encountering fog and rain, but experiencing fresh breezes from the north and west and cloudiness at noon of that fateful Wednesday. At 2 p.m., a sail was spied to the southward and *Constitution* went in chase. At 3 p.m., it was identified as a full-rigged ship on a starboard tack. Thirty minutes later, Hull knew he had come upon a frigate.

At 3:45 p.m., the chase lay her main topsail to the mast, a clear invitation to duel. But Isaac Hull was not one to rush into things. He ordered the topgallant sails, stay sails, and flying jib taken in, the courses hauled up, a second reef taken in the topsails, and the royal yards sent down. Upon beating to quarters, his crew gave three cheers. According to Seaman Moses Smith, the legend "NOT THE LITTLE BELT" could be seen painted on one of the enemy's topsails, a reference to the British war brig which had been shattered by *Constitution* 's near-sister *President* in a night encounter the year before the war began.

A half hour later, at 4:10 p.m., when about one mile separated the opposing frigates, the enemy hoisted three blue British ensigns and "discharged her Starboard Broadside at us without effect. She immediately wore round, and discharged her Larboard Broadside two shot of which rubbed us and the remainder flying over and through our rigging, we then hoisted our Ensigns and Jack, at the Fore and Main Top Gallant Mastheads." Each time the enemy fired, Hull altered course to disturb her gunners' aim, first to larboard and then to starboard.[1] A British ball struck abaft the larboard knighthead at one point, showering splinters without effect. The American crew fired it back. Another struck the foremast, cutting a hoop in two. The American fired only when and as individual guns could be brought to bear.

After some forty-five minutes of inconclusive maneuvering, the Briton, impatient at Hull's reticence to close from his upwind position, bore up with the wind "rather on his Lab'd Quarter," a maneuver calculated to be seen as an invitation to close for a toe-to-toe slugfest, one Isaac Hull accepted. Setting his maintopgallant sail, he moved in, his gun crews standing alert, double-shotting their guns with solid and grape shot for a full broadside. Another British ball came aboard, the concussion from which knocked Seaman Isaac Kingman down, but not out.

Hull was where he wanted to be at about 5 p.m.. He hauled down his jib and laid the main topsail shivering to slow down as he ranged up alongside. Reportedly at his command, "Now, boys, hull her!," the first double-shotted broadside crashed out at the Briton half a pistol shot distance to larboard. Blast followed blast. The Captain is said to have split his breeches, jumping up and down in the excitement. Approximately fifteen minutes later, the Briton's mizzenmast crashed over the starboard side; her main yard was shot from its slings. "Huzza boys! We've made a brig of her! Next time we'll make her a sloop!" The American crew gave three cheers and went on firing.

The return fire from the British frigate had generally been high, in accordance with their practice of seeking to dismast an opponent. Some of *Constitution*'s braces were slashed and her fore royal truck was shot away, together with two halyards - one bearing one of the flags Hull had hoisted. Amidst the cannonade, Seaman Daniel Hogan climbed the rigging and made it fast to the topmast. British shot hitting the hull made little impression. Someone saw a ball hit, make a dent, then fall into the sea, and he cried out, "Huzza! Her sides are made of iron!" And so the famed nickname "Old Ironsides" was born.

The dragging wreckage, jammed as it was up under his starboard counter, slowed the Briton, pulled his head to starboard, and allowed *Constitution* to begin drawing ahead. The British Captain tried in vain to regain control of his ship's head. At the same time, Hull attempted to luff up across his bow and rake, "but our braces being shot away and Jib haulyards [sic], we could not effect it" - at least not as planned. The British frigate, swinging rapidly to starboard, crashed into *Constitution*'s larboard quarter, smashing the boat in the davits and snagging his bowsprit in the larboard mizzen shrouds. Hitting and recoiling as the American slid forward, before breaking clear astern the Briton's bowsprit wreaked havoc with Hull's gig in the stern davits.

The record goes momentarily blank at this point. Given the fact that Hull had never before been in a ship-to-ship battle in any

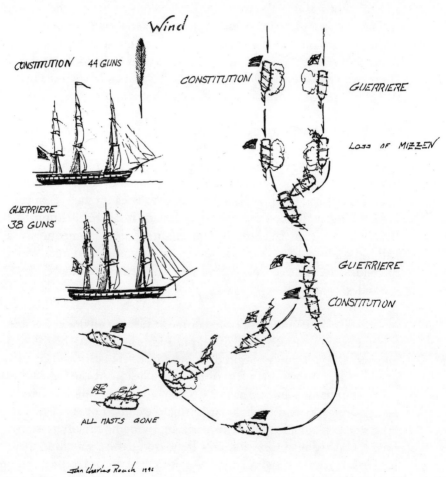

Wind

CONSTITUTION 44 GUNS

CONSTITUTION

GUERRIERE

LOSS OF MIZZEN

GUERRIERE
38 GUNS

GUERRIERE

CONSTITUTION

ALL MASTS GONE

John Charles Roach 1996

capacity, let alone command, and suddenly faced with a crippled enemy and finding his own maneuvering capability impaired, it is fair to assume that there was some confusion and momentary indecision. How long it took Hull to regain control of the situation and exactly what he did was not recorded either by Hull or his subordinates. His enemies, busy with their own problems, stated merely that he took up a position off their larboard bow from whence he fired several broadsides into them to which they could only weakly respond.

Satisfied that the British frigate still was not under control, Hull moved to take a raking position ahead of her. For some reason - miscalculation, bungled sail-handling, or unexpected movement of the enemy ship - instead of passing clear ahead, the antagonists collided, *Constitution* taking her enemy's jibboom in her starboard mizzen shrouds. The crash destroyed the American's spanker gaff and boom, and snapped off the starboard half of the crossjack yard, as she unleashed two broadsides into his bow. The Briton's flying jibboom and jibboom were carried away, and his two ragged shots in reply killed two and wounded one at Gun #15 starboard in Hull's cabin, and started a brief blaze.

This unexpected and unplanned opportunity to board the enemy left both opponents scrambling for the advantage. First Lieutenant William S. Bush, commanding the American Marines, leaped to the taffrail to lead the charge and was killed instantly by a musket ball in the face. He was the first American Marine officer to die in combat in service of his country. Charles Morris, Hull's second in command, sought to replace him but was downed, shot through the abdomen. The even heavier American musketry killed the British Second Lieutenant, and wounded the Captain, First Lieutenant, and Sailing Master. Before a further attempt could be made, *Constitution*'s forward motion exerted sufficient force to pull the ships apart. The resultant whipping action in the Briton's bowsprit was transmitted through the stays to a weakened foremast, which crashed down to starboard, its plunging weight causing the tottering mainmast to follow it.

Hull, seeing his enemy thus completely immobilized, stood eastward with fore and main courses and a reef in his topsails, keeping his target silhouetted against the lowering sun. The crew set busily to reeving new braces and halyards, and readying the ship to resume the action. When these immediate repairs were done, he returned to find the shattered Briton had only the bedraggled remnants of the spritsail yard remaining. Unseen by Hull were the 18-pounder long guns on the enemy's gun deck that had been torn loose from their tackles and were running amok as the ship rolled her ports under in the heavy swells. The British Captain wisely fired a gun to leeward in token of submission as the Yankee frigate came within a mile. Hull made the appropriate response - one gun - and this most decisive ship action was over. It was shortly before 7 p.m. Wrote Surgeon Evans:

"Our crew behaved very nobly. They fought like heroes, and gave three cheers when the colours were hoisted. They also cheered when each of her masts went over the side, and when her colours were struck."

Third Lieutenant George Campbell Read was sent first to take possession of the vanquished. At 7:30 p.m., all boats were hoisted out to bring prisoners aboard, to take aid to the wounded, and to pass a towing hawser. Twenty-two-year-old Midshipman Henry Gilliam was among those with Read, and he later wrote to his uncle that he had found the decks littered with "pieces of skulls, brains, legs, arms & blood ...in every directions [sic] and groanes [sic] of the wounded were almost enough to make me curse the war." Adding a bizarre note to this gory scene was the presence of molasses splattered on everything, the surviving reminder of a cask of the stuff ordered up beforehand by the British Captain in preparation for taunting the defeated Yankees with switchel, a rum concoction favored by them. At 8, a boat returned to *Constitution* with the first of the prisoners. Principal among them was Captain James Richard Dacres, Royal Navy, late commander of His British Majesty's Frigate *Guerriere*.

James Dacres came from a Navy family (his father had commanded *HMS Carleton* in the Battle of Valcour Island against Americans in 1776) and had entered the service at an early age, attaining his rank of Lieutenant in 1804. In 1805, he was posted to command of the sloop of war *Elk* and the following year to command of the frigate *Bacchante*, 24 guns, on the Jamaica Station. In this post, he served with distinction. He took command of *Guerriere* about April 1811.

Dacres' ship was French-built and had been rated by them at 50 guns. She had been taken by the British off Norway in 1806, and after a two-year refit was commissioned by them as "5th rate, large 38." On 19 August 1812, she was armed with thirty 18-pounders on the gun deck, fourteen 32-pounder carronades and one 12-pounder howitzer on her quarterdeck, and two 12-pounders and two 32-pounder carronades on the forecastle - forty-nine guns in all. At the time of the engagement she was due for refit in Halifax. Her hull was fouled and there was rot in her masts; her rigging, badly worn.

*Constitution*'s battery at this time consisted of thirty 24-pounders on the gun deck, sixteen 32-pounder carronades on the quarterdeck, one 18-pounder and eight 32-pounder carronades on the forecastle - a total of 55 guns. She had completed a thorough refit only two months earlier.

The *Constitution-Guerriere* fight was a straight-forward, toe-to-toe battle between two adversaries each confident in his abilities. *Constitution* was the bigger, heavier, and because of her recent yard period, the faster. But as this fight was a slugfest, this last advantage was not a factor. Indeed, with his green crew, Hull may have decided on the direct approach, hoping to minimize having to maneuver and fight simultaneously. He fought a graceless fight, relying on his size advantage to compensate for his inexperience and that of his crew.

In terms of gun power, there was less disparity in the respective broadsides than the simple number of guns and their calibers would indicate. The French-made shot used by *Guerriere* generally was somewhat heavier than its stated size - about eight percent, on the average. American shot, on the other hand, ran about seven percent light. Taking this into account, and without considering *Guerriere*'s howitzer (of little moment), the resultant broadside weights were 581 pounds (British) and 692 pounds (American). But the greater result stemmed from the Americans' lower aim and the *Guerriere*'s lighter construction. *Guerriere*'s wreckage topside was more visible and of consequence in the short term, but the damage below was irreparable: about thirty American shot had hulled her below the waterline, according to Captain Dacres. By contrast, *Constitution*'s hull damage largely was limited to the mess created in the starboard portion of Hull's cabin when the two ships entangled the second time.[2] Dacres' guns, however, *had* done considerable damage to Hull's standing and running rigging, and spars. In addition to shot away braces and halyards, both fore and main masts had been shot through, as was the heel of the foretopgallant mast; and the band for the main slings had been broken. Clearly, the larger dimensions of the masts contributed to their survival. In addition, the crossjack had been snapped and the gaff, spanker boom, and gig smashed, as had the larboard quarter boat.

  *Constitution* carried a much larger crew than did *Guerriere* - about 450 versus 275-300 - which rendered the superb service of her guns possible.[3] Moreover, Hull had trained his men daily in the aiming and loading of their guns. Their rate of fire was abetted by the use, in part, of lead foil powder cylinders which reduced the need to swab guns out after each shot. The British, on the other hand, were handicapped by the fact that their twenty-year-old war with France had put such a premium on their powder supply as largely to preclude the use of powder merely for training purposes in their vastly expanded navy. Even so, this was the first frigate duel they had lost since 1803. The morale of the American crew, as well, was superior: the Britons in it, too, were willing to fight. The Americans in *Guerriere*'s crew, on the other hand, protested having to do so, and Dacres gallantly sent them below as noncombatants. Twenty-three Britons died as a result of the action, and another fifty-six were wounded; Hull had had seven killed and a like number wounded.[4] (Eight surviving British crew members subsequently claimed political asylum when landed in Boston, and two signed on board "Old Ironsides.")

  Before resuming our narrative, it seems at this point proper to ponder the effect of Fortune in this battle. What would have been the outcome if Dacres had succeeded in raking *Constitution* from astern instead of suffering the first collision? Might not he have downed one or both of the masts already damaged? Might not have *Constitution*'s steering gear been destroyed? And might not Hull then have been in the position, in a largely immobilized ship, of making the difficult decision of whether or not more blood gainfully could be shed? John Paul Jones abandoned his sinking *Bon Homme Richard* for the newly surrendered *Serapis* in 1779. James Dacres might have stepped from a dying *Guerriere* to *Constitution* if Fortune had been his that day in 1812. The British Captain himself was sensitive to this, for he subsequently stated:*

    "...I am so aware that the success of my opponent
    was owing to fortune, that it is my earnest wish, and it
    would be the happiest period of my life, to be once more
    opposed to the *Constitution*...in a frigate of similar force
    to the *Guerriere*," with the same crew.

To return to our narrative.

For three hours, the Americans attempted to take their prize in tow. By 11 P. M., however, it was evident that the differing drift rates of the two ships and the difficulties of working in darkness made it an almost impossible task. The hawser was cast off. Hull kept *Constitution* "at a convenient distance" from *Guerriere* through the night, while Lieutenant Read and his prize crew struggled to keep her afloat. In the American frigate, repairs were begun. Both Surgeons, Evans and Irwin (of *Guerriere*), worked to save the wounded. Evans himself did four amputations.

At 7 a.m. on the morning of the 20 August, *Constitution*'s foretopgallant yard and the damaged foretopgallant mast were sent down, and a new mast stepped. Elsewhere, the carpenters were preparing fishes (splints) for the damaged fore and main masts.

As the foretopgallant yard was being sent up at 7:30 a.m., Lieutenant Read hailed from *Guerriere* that she had five feet of water in the hold and that it was gaining on them. Hull decided to withdraw his men and destroy the hulk. By 1:30 p.m., everyone was off except for Read and his demolition party. They left for *Constitution* at 3 p.m.

Moses Smith has described *Guerriere*'s last moments:

"There was something melancholy and grand in the sight. Although the frigate was a wreck, floating about a mastless hulk at the sport of the waves, she bore marks of her former greatness. Much of her ornamental work had been untouched; and her long, high, black sides rose in solitary majesty before us, as we bade her farewell... [H]er years were now ended; her course was run; she was about to sink into the deep ocean forever.

"Captain Dacres stood by our taffrail as we squared away from the *Guerriere*...

"At the distance of about three miles we hove to and awaited the result. Hundreds of eyes were stretched in that one direction, where the ill-fated *Guerriere* moved heavily on the deep. It was like waiting for the uncapping of a volcano — or the

19

bursting up of a crater. Scarcely a word was spoken on board the *Constitution*, so breathless was the interest felt in the scene.

"The first intimation we had that the fire was at work was the discharge of the guns. One after another, as the flame advanced, they came booming toward us. Roar followed roar, flash followed flash, until the whole mass was enveloped in clouds of smoke. We could see but little of the direct progress of the work, and therefore we looked more earnestly for the explosion — not knowing how soon it might occur. Presently there was a dead silence; then followed a vibratory, shuddering motion, and streams of light, like streaks of lightning running along the sides; and the grand crash came! The quarter deck, which was immediately over the magazine, lifted in a mass, broke into fragments, and flew in every direction. The hull, parted in the center by the shock, and loaded with such masses of iron and spars, reeled, staggered, plunged forward a few feet, and sank out of sight.

"It was a grand and awful scene. Nearly every floating thing around her went down with the *Guerriere*... We immediately squared away, and were again under a crowd of sail for our native land."

It was 3:15 P. M., 20 August 1812, and Isaac Hull was eager to broadcast news of his triumph. At 6 p.m., he beat to quarters and mustered his crew. Lieutenant Bush and one of the British seamen who had failed to survive his wounds were buried with proper ceremony. That done, sail was set for Boston, where they arrived on 30 August.

With the battle done and *Constitution* safely in home port, it is an appropriate moment to consider the background of the adulation that shortly was to engulf Hull and his men, and the effect their victory was to have on future events. As has been stated previously, the declaration of war was unpopular in several regions of the country, but particularly so in New England. It was thought that nothing good would come of it. Trade would be interrupted or destroyed, insurance rates would rise, and ships lost through destruction or capture. At sea, the Royal Navy had been well nigh invincible in nearly two decades of warfare against the might of Napoleon. The minuscule United States Navy would be swallowed whole - almost without notice.

The nautical negativism was reinforced by a disaster on land: on 16 August, after some indecisive maneuvering the American forces at Detroit had surrendered without a fight to an inferior force of British and Indian allies. This news had only recently become known in Boston, just long enough to depress morale further. (Ironically, the American general involved was William Hull, Isaac's uncle.)

Thus, the stage was set and the nation ready - craving - for good news. *Constitution*'s victory over *Guerriere* was all that. The fight had been decisive. *Guerriere* apparently had been destroyed with expedition and with minimum loss of life and ship damage. The mighty Royal Navy had been humbled by an upstart. A Son of Liberty again had tweaked George's royal nose.

Hull got all the adulation and celebration he wanted in response to giving the nation the victory for which it hungered. The Secretary responded to the news on 9 September saying, "...we know not which most to applaud, Your gallantry or Your skill — You, Your officers & Crew are entitled to & will receive the applause & the gratitude of Your gratefull country." Numerous lithographs based on the Corne` paintings were reproduced and snapped up by an eager public. Plays were written and songs sung. Congress voted Hull a gold medal, his officers silver ones, and $50,000 for all hands to share in lieu of prize money.[5] Lieutenant Charles Morris was meritoriously promoted to Captain.[6] New York, Philadelphia, Charleston, and his home state of Connecticut vied with each other in presenting Hull with rich tokens of their esteem. Above all, the victory became a bench mark, a touchstone, the symbol of all that was good and right with the American way. Perhaps the most perceptive evaluation ever written appeared in the London *Times* when the bad news reached England:

"It is not merely that an English frigate has been taken, after, what we are free to confess, may be called a brave resistance, but that it has been taken by a new enemy, an enemy unaccustomed to such triumphs, and likely to be rendered insolent and confident by them. He must be a weak politician who does not see how

important the first triumph is in giving a tone and
character to the war. Never before in the history of
the world did an English frigate strike to an American ..."[7]

In Boston town, the evaluation made up in verve what it lacked in
polish:

"The *Constitution* long shall be
The glory of our Navy,
For when she grapples with a foe,
She sends him to old Davy.
Yankee doodle keep it up,
Yankee doodle dandy,
We'll let the British know that we
At fighting are quite handy."

# NOTES:

1. Hull's yawing first one way and then the other to avoid being raked was interpreted by Dacres as being attempts by his enemy to gain a raking position astern of him, hence the repeated reversals of course and alternating broadsides. In other words, each was trying to prevent what the other, in fact, was not attempting to do.

2. *Guerriere*'s maximum hull thickness was perhaps one-third less than *Constitution*'s twenty-one inches.

3. *Constitution* expended 300 24-pounder round shot, 236 32-pounder round shot, ten 18-pounder round shot, 140 stands of 32-pounder grape, 120 stands of 24-pounder grape, 40 24-pounder canister, 60 32-pounder cannister, and 47 24-pounder double-headed shot. All told, 953 shot and 2376 pounds of black powder. In itself, the amount expended is an indication that the battle lasted longer than the thirty-five minutes of close action Hull implied in his reports.

4. One of the American dead, Robert Brice, had failed to swab out his quarterdeck carronade properly and was lost when it went off prematurely.

5. If Congress had acted more precipitately, Hull and crew would have received $100,000. As it was, news of victories by Commodore Bainbridge (to be related next), Captain Stephen Decatur and Captain Jacob Jones arrived in time to put things in perspective. The sum of $125,000 was voted to be divided with two-fifths each going to Hull and Bainbridge, and one-fifth to Jones. Decatur, who managed to bring his victim home for acceptance into the Navy, shared $200,000 with his crew. Charles W. Goldsborough acted as prize agent for the *Constitution*s, and in seven weeks in 1813 visited Boston, Portsmouth (NH), New York, Philadelphia, and Baltimore, paying former crewmen in each place before returning to Washington. As of 7 October 1818, he still had $3116 to be disbursed.

6. Morris' promotion to Captain, bypassing the rank of Master Commandant, was Secretary of the Navy Paul Hamilton's decision. He, however, left office before a storm of letters from outraged officers climaxed. The Senate narrowly gave its assent just before its term ended in March 1813, preserving Hamilton's dignity, but directed that never again was an officer to be promoted *two* grades, no matter how heroic his act.

7. The article went on to say, "...and we cannot say, that capt. Dacres, under all circumstances, is punishable for this act; yet we do say, there are commanders in the English navy, who would a thousand times have rather gone down with their colors flying, then [sic] have set their brother officers so fatal an example."

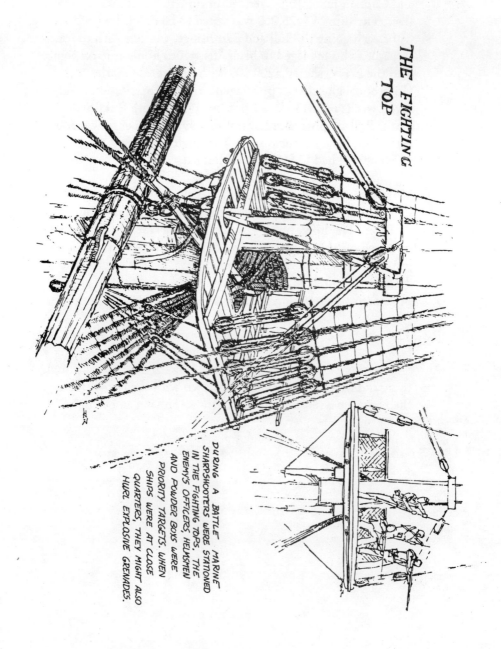

## THE FIGHTING TOP

DURING A BATTLE MARINE
SHARPSHOOTERS WERE STATIONED
IN THE FIGHTING TOPS. THE
ENEMY'S OFFICERS, HELMSMEN
AND POWDER BOYS WERE
PRIORITY TARGETS. WHEN
SHIPS WERE AT CLOSE
QUARTERS, THEY MIGHT ALSO
HURL EXPLOSIVE GRENADES.

# PART II

A sad note was Hull's in this moment of triumph when he learned that his brother in New York had died during his absence, leaving a widow and children. Hull confided in Commodore Bainbridge, Commandant of the Navy Yard, that he intended that very day to request a shore assignment in order to settle his brother's affairs and provide for his family. Bainbridge, who had been seeking a combat command, and had expected to relieve Hull in early August, promptly wrote to Secretary Hamilton suggesting that he and Hull exchange commands.

On 7 September, overhaul work on *Constitution* began in earnest. On 14 September, Bainbridge received the Secretary's response to his request to succeed Hull; it was in the affirmative. Bainbridge moved swiftly and took command at 4 o'clock the next afternoon, hoisting his broad blue pennant as a squadron commander.

William Bainbridge was in command of *Philadelphia* when she grounded and was lost to the Tripoline pirates in October of 1803. A native of New Jersey, Bainbridge had entered merchant marine service in 1789, at the age of 15, and had earned his first command only four years later. With the reestablishment of the Navy in 1798, he was commissioned a Lieutenant Commandant and given the schooner *Retaliation*, the former French privateer *Le Croyable*. He shortly was captured without firing a shot by a superior French force, the first officer in the United States Navy to surrender his command to an enemy. Bainbridge was absolved of any blame, promoted to Master Commandant, and given command of the brig *Norfolk*, wherein he had some success in the West Indies. In 1800, then commanding the light frigate *George Washington*, Bainbridge was finessed by the Dey of Algiers into making a trip to Constantinople for him in his ship but *under the Algerine flag*. This was the first time an American warship was seen at the Porte, and Bainbridge made a very favorable impression despite the circumstance which had brought him there. Bainbridge subsequently commanded frigate *Essex*, 32 guns, in Commodore Dale's squadron before returning to the Mediterranean in *Philadelphia*. Following his release from Tripoli in 1805 he again was cleared of any negligence, but requested and received permission to leave service temporarily to return to the merchant marine. In 1808, believing that war was imminent with Britain, Bainbridge voluntarily returned to active duty in command of *President*. But when war didn't come right away, he again became a merchant captain. In February of 1812, he had once more presented himself for service to Secretary Hamilton and, in accordance with his wishes, was given a shore command until such time as war broke out, when he would be given a ship. Such was *Constitution*'s new Captain.

Surgeon Evans has left a description of the change of command:

"...The crew expressed publicly much dissatisfaction at the change, in consequence of which the Armourer was put in confinement on board the Gun Boat [No. 85] for trial. They gave Capt. H. three hearty cheers as he left the ship. The scene altogether affecting. The whole crew had a great affection for him. They urged him to remain: said they would go out with him and take the Africa [the British ship of the line]: & finally requested to be transferred on board any other vessel. On being asked by Capt. B., who it was that had ever sailed with him & refused to go again, several persons spoke — one man said he had sailed with him in the Phila. & had been badly used — that it might be altered now, but he would prefer going with Capt. H. or any of the other commanders. Several others said they had sailed with him before, and did not wish to sail again..."

Obviously, this victorious crew viewed Bainbridge as a three-time loser and wanted no part of him. The 38-year-old Bainbridge, on the other hand, inwardly shaken by his reception, unsuccessfully offered Commodore John Rodgers $5000 to exchange his flagship *President* for *Constitution*.

Bainbridge's main concern in readying the ship for sea was, of course, ensuring that all spar and rigging damage suffered in the recent engagement was repaired or replaced. For the next month, the log records the tedious labor of erecting the shears alongside the mainmast and removing it, and of stepping a new one. Then the process was repeated for the foremast. With that accomplished, the fighting tops had to be set back atop these lower masts, the topmasts fidded home, the trestletrees installed, the topgallant masts stepped, and all the rigging rereeved. Of course, a new gaff and spanker boom, and crossjack yard, also were put aboard.

On 16 October, Bainbridge moved *Constitution* from the Navy Yard to a position off Long Wharf to complete loading. Five days later, he moved again to an anchorage in President Roads, from whence he could take advantage of a fair wind. *Hornet*, the second unit of his squadron, moved to the same locale on 24 October. Both wind and tide came fair on the 27th, and the two ships stood for the open sea. Bainbridge's orders were to take frigate *Essex* (32, Captain David Porter) and brig *Hornet* (18, Master Commandant James Lawrence) and "to annoy the enemy and to afford protection to our commerce, pursuing that course, which to your best judgment may ... appear to be best." The Commodore already had considered this aspect of his orders and had decided to proceed first to waters off the Cape Verde Islands, then in a southwesterly direction, touching on many of the principal sea lanes used by both sides, and then farther south to the waters off Brazil, where the British at that time had considerable commerce. After two months on that coast, he intended then to proceed to the vicinity of St. Helena Island, which was frequented by British East Indiamen returning home. (*Essex*, which was in the Delaware when Bainbridge sailed, ultimately never rendezvoused with him, Porter pursuing instead an option in his orders: to disrupt British maritime activities in the Pacific. This he accomplished with legendary success before finally being trapped and captured in Valparaiso, Chile.)

The ships were in the vicinity of the Cape Verde Islands on 19 November when Surgeon Evans engaged in a little amusement and

> "...Threw a bottle overboard today with the intention of ascertaining the current. It contains a piece of paper on which was written the Latitude, Longitude, date, & my name, with a request that the finder would make it public. The paper was oiled. The bottle corked, sealed, & a piece of Tarrd muslin tied over it..."

We'll never know if it ever was found.

Landfall was made on the Brazilian coast on 6 December. *Constitution* and *Hornet* proceeded southward along the coast, periodically closing enough to catch sight of land. A few native craft were seen, and one Portuguese brig involved in local trade was boarded, before they arrived in the area of Sao Salvador (now Bahia). Not wishing to reveal his whole strength, on the evening of 13 December Bainbridge ordered Lawrence in to the port to contact the American Consul and gain the latest intelligence.

*Hornet* returned in the midafternoon of the 18th, and Lawrence boarded the flagship immediately to report. In harbor, he had found *HMS Bonne Citoyenne*, 18 guns, a war sloop repairing a leak caused by a grounding. The sleek, red-sided vessel was said to be carrying $1,600,000 in specie to England, From Consul Henry Hill he had learned that there was a British ship of the line, *Montague*, 74, at Rio, and two other lesser units farther south. Only one man-of-war was said to be near St. Helena. Unfortunately, at the moment *Bonne Citoyenne* was the only Briton in the harbor.

After receiving the stores brought out by Lawrence, *Constitution* and *Hornet* spent the next few days patrolling to the north and south of the port looking for prizes without success. On the 23rd, a sail was sighted close inshore making for the port, but Bainbridge's meticulous orders respecting Portuguese sovereignty precluded her capture by Lawrence, who nonetheless followed her into port. While there, he issued a challenge to Captain Pitt Barnaby Greene of *Bonne Citoyenne* to fight him, ship to ship, with *Constitution* pledged to remain aloof regardless of the outcome. Greene steadfastly refused - and rightly so, with all that gold aboard - despite acrimonious assaults on his character by the challenger and Bainbridge. Bainbridge further was angered by a hard-line letter from the Governor of Sao Salvador complaining about the repeated entries into port by *Hornet*. The Portuguese clearly was showing his British bias. Bainbridge ordered *Hornet* to remain guarding *Bonne Citoyenne* and to take her the minute she left port and cleared territorial waters. He took *Constitution* offshore to cruise for prizes.

Between 8 and 9 in the morning of 29 December, a Tuesday, while some thirty miles off the coast, two strange sail were made out inshore (to the northwest) and to windward (to the northeast). The former was seen to continue her course along the coast while the other, the larger one, altered course toward *Constitution*. Bainbridge already had tacked in their direction. The day was pleasant and the sea nearly calm; the wind was light from the eastnortheast.

By 11 a.m., Commodore Bainbridge and his officers believed that the windward contact was a British ship of the line. He tacked *Constitution* to the southeast to avoid being pinned into pro-British Brazilian territorial waters by a larger adversary.[1] The American frigate was sailing close to the wind with her royals set.

At noon, *Constitution* showed her colors, and the opponent shortly thereafter set a red British ensign. He then flew a series of signals, the appropriate recognition signals for British, Spanish, and Portuguese warships, but of course got no response from the American.

Bainbridge realized that the contact was but a frigate at about 1:20 p.m., when it was certain she was closing, something no liner could do on a frigate in those conditions. He tacked toward the enemy, taking in his mainsail and royals. When slightly more than a mile separated them, he tacked again. Both ships now were heading southeast, with the Briton to windward on Bainbridge's larboard quarter and coming up. Clearly, she had the speed advantage.

At this point, the enemy hauled down his ensign, although his jack remained aloft. The Commodore ordered his 24-pounders to commence broadside firing aimed at the target's rigging when the range had decreased to about a thousand yards — at nearly the maxi-

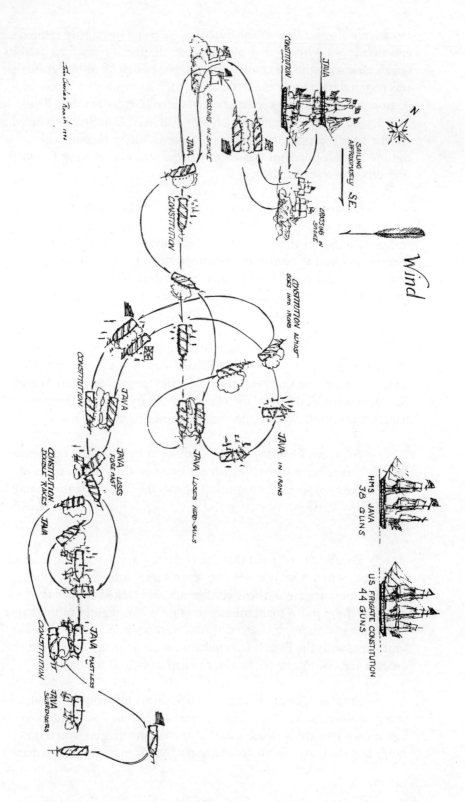

mum effective range of those guns and beyond that of anything the enemy had. Apparently, his intention was to try and at least slow her down, if not stop her before she could outspeed him and bring her guns to bear. He was not successful. The enemy held his fire until within range, at about 2 p.m., and the battle was joined, both sides firing furiously. The Briton's first salvos were the most damaging, *Constitution*'s spars and rigging being well chewed and Bainbridge wounded in the thigh. Amidst the hail of iron, Seaman Asa Curtis slid down the American's foretopgallant stay to "rebend the Flying Jib Halyards which had been shot away," thereby preventing the loss of an important head sail. The enemy frigate forged ahead and appeared to be about to cross *Constitution*'s bow for a devastating rake when Bainbridge loosed a broadside, then masterfully wore around in the smoke. It was 2:10 p.m.. The enemy followed suit, but was once again left on the windward quarter - this time, to starboard. Again the enemy drew alongside and then ahead, seeking to achieve a raking position. And yet again, at 2:25 p.m., Bainbridge fired and wore in the smoke, denying the advantage. The ships once more were heading generally southeastward.

The faster frigate a third time came up on *Constitution*'s quarter and appeared to be drawing ahead when, suddenly, she wore and cut under the American's stern, unleashing a killing raking broadside at 2:35 p.m. *Constitution*'s wheel disappeared in a cloud of splinters, all four helmsmen down. Eleven members of carronade crews were dropped. And the Commodore had been hit again in the thigh. It must have been a desperate moment for him, in pain and shocky, the remembrance of his three former failures in mind. He steeled himself and, using a midshipman aide for support, began issuing orders setting up a jury rigged steering system down below with several midshipmen to relay orders.

While the Americans were thus engaged, the bemused enemy, unaware of the critical damage done, expected the American to turn to starboard and parallel his course. When, instead, *Constitution* was seen sailing steadily off, it was assumed she had had enough. The British frigate was tacked back across her wake and another raking broadside fired at rather long range. Then she tacked again having regained the weather gauge, and began hauling forward to larboard. Bainbridge set fore and main courses and steered still closer to the wind, now hoping to bring his carronades with their smashing power into play and inflict some crippling damage before his own situation worsened. His gamble paid off. At about 2:40 p.m. his foe's bowsprit cap, jib boom, and headsails were shot away. Seeing *Constitution* beginning to wear again, the British Captain, denied the use of his headsails to drive his bow off the wind, decided instead to tack across the wind using his spanker to drive the stern into the turn. It didn't work, and, like an airplane stalling at the top of a climb, his ship hung up heading into the wind, temporarily "in irons" — unable to maneuver. Seeing this, Bainbridge continued to wear *his* ship through nearly three-quarters of a circle to starboard, picking up enough speed to close his enemy's larboard quarter and get in a murderous rake himself at 2:50 p.m. before he had to wear to larboard to keep his ship under control. *Constitution* swung back to the original heading, the enemy following once he had forced his bow around.

The two frigates now ran off to the southeast, the Briton still having the weather gauge. But the advantage was seen by both sides to be shifting to the Americans. British gunfire was becoming less accurate than it had been during those first broadsides that had taken the greatest toll in Americans. Her loss of headsails with the destruction of the jibboom made the British frigate less maneuverable, offsetting in part *Constitution*'s lack of a wheel and slower speed. The British Captain decided his best tactic was to close and take his adversary by boarding before even that opportunity was lost. Accordingly, at 3:35 p.m. he sought to run down on *Constitution*'s larboard main chains. A misjudgment on his part resulted in the remains of his bowsprit running into the American's mizzen rigging and momentarily hanging him up. There, with only one of his guns able to bear, he had to suffer the full weight of *Constitution*'s metal and the hail of musketry from her well-trained Marines. The enemy's foremast was severed just below its fighting top and plunged through two decks; then his main topmast went, cut off slightly above the cap. The resulting tangle of wreckage further disorganized his gun crews. The enemy Captain was dropped by an American sharpshooter.[2]

As they separated, both ships brought their heads eastward once more. *Constitution*, now having the weather gauge, began forereaching her battered antagonist. Bainbridge wore yet again at 3:50 p.m. and brought his ship across the opponent's bow, where he loosed a blazing raking fire. Crossing southward, he continued to wear until he crossed astern on a northerly heading at 4:13 p.m. and raked again with his starboard batteries before falling off to larboard and coming back around to take up a position on his opponent's starboard quarter, where he kept station and banged away while the enemy was unable to bring guns to bear on him. When the Briton's main yard was shot in the slings and her spanker shot away, she slowed down and Bainbridge slid forward to an abeam position. Before the Americans could set more sail, the Britons were able to shoot back with the three to five guns still operational on that side. The enemy's remaining section of foremast just above the spar deck was shot away, and at about 4:55 p.m., "Shott Away his Mizen Mast Nearly to the Deck." All this time the enemy had attempted to return *Constitution*'s devastating fire, but the tangled wreckage encumbering his starboard side flamed each time he shot. His cannons went still one by one until, shortly after 5 p.m., silence reigned. His colors having disappeared from the main rigging, Commodore Bainbridge assumed his opponent had surrendered, and he took his ship off to windward a short distance to affect necessary repairs before closing and taking possession. The time was 5:10 p.m.

But the fact was the Briton had not surrendered. First Lieutenant Henry Ducie Chads had assumed command upon the wounding of his Captain, and strove mightily to prepare for further fighting. A staysail was rigged between a topmast jury rigged to replace the foremast and the bowsprit in an effort to bring the ship under some control. When he tried to rig a sail of sorts on the half of the main yard still aloft, the damaged mainmast - at least, the remaining lower mast - tottered and had to be dropped to keep it from doing worse damage. When *Constitution* began to close once more, a half-hour later, the British had rehoisted an ensign to the mizzen stump and were trying to set more sail. Seeing that the American was taking an unassailable raking position across his bow, the British Lieutenant wisely hauled down his flag, only just barely in time to prevent another broadside. It was 5:50 p.m.. In *Constitution*, recalling the fight against *Guerriere*, the "crew gave 3 cheers, as they had done when we first beat to quarters & several times during the action." Bainbridge had his victory at last.[3]

At 6:00 p.m., George Parker, who had succeeded the recuperating Charles Morris as First Lieutenant, boarded the defeated enemy from one of *Constitution*'s two remaining undamaged boats (out of *eight*) to find a shambles. Four of his forecastle guns were upended and so were six more on the quarterdeck. Tangled rigging was everywhere. The wounded and dying made it a grisly scene. The scene was repeated on the gun deck below. The defeated frigate was *HMS Java*,

38, the former French *Renomée*, commissioned in the Royal Navy only the previous August. She had sailed from England for India on 12 November and had detoured to Sao Salvador because of a shortage of water. Quite similar to *Guerriere*, she carried twenty-eight 18-pounder long guns below, and two long 9-pounders, sixteen 32-pounder and one 18-pounder carronades on her forecastle and quarter-deck, a total of forty-seven guns. (Bainbridge had made a small change in his ship's armament since her last fight, removing the 18-pounder chase gun - leaving fifty-four guns, in all.) *Java*'s gunfire, devastating in its opening broadsides, had diminished steadily in accuracy and volume as the fight progressed, symptomatic not only of damage received but the presence of a new crew that had been allowed to fire but six blank cartridges in practice.

*Constitution* suffered nine killed and twenty-five wounded (five mortally) out of her crew of 480.[4] Conflicting reports by several present make it impossible to be precise concerning *Java*. She had somewhere between 373 and 426 people on board at the time of the fight. Deaths were reported as totaling between twenty-two and sixty, while the wounded were numbered at either 101 or 102. In any event, the disparate ratio of 4 or 5 to 1 in casualties between the two ships is indicative of the volume and power of the American fire compared to her enemy's.

The unusually large number of people in *Java* stems from the fact that she was carrying nearly a hundred passengers out to their new duty assignments in and around India, including the Governor General-designate of Bombay, Lieutenant General Sir Thomas Hislop.

The wrecked condition of *Java* already has been noted. On the American side, *Constitution* once again had come through without crippling damage but had not escaped entirely unscathed. Careful scrutiny of the ship's log for the succeeding days discloses that both fore and mizzen masts were "wounded" severely enough to warrant fishes, as did certain of the yards. Additionally, the maintopmast had to be taken down and replaced. Thus, it would seem that the slightly larger dimensions of "Old Ironsides'" masts had saved her - narrowly - from the fate suffered by her two opponents to date.

Considering his own "damaged" condition, the weakened state of his ship's spars and rigging, the fact that he was thousands of miles from home in waters infested with the enemy, Bainbridge reluctantly determined to destroy *Java* rather than attempt to tow her home. Slowly - very slowly, with only two boats available - the prisoners were brought aboard and distributed about the spar and gun decks of *Constitution* under guard of American Marines, the enlisted men manacled to preclude an uprising. Last to be transferred was *Java*'s mortally wounded Captain, Henry Lambert, one of England's finest frigate captains, whose green, nondescript crew had not been equal to his tactical skill. It was a terribly painful move across choppy waters, but was made with all the care and tenderness possible. By noon on the final day of 1812, all people and personal gear were clear and the demolition fires set. At 3 p.m., she blew up. Noted Surgeon Evans: "The explosion was not so grand as that of the *Guerriere*, as her small Magazine only took fire." The was at least the fourth scuttling he had witnessed; he was becoming an expert on the subject. Bainbridge made sail for Sao Salvador.

At 8:30 a.m. on New Year's morning, land and a sail were sighted ahead. On the chance it might be *Montague* or another enemy warship, the prisoners were herded below and confined in the hold, and the ship beat to quarters. In the heat and closeness of their confinement, the British suffered considerable discomfort - particularly the wounded. This act was to bring the wrath of some British observers down on Bainbridge's head, with charges of cruelty and malice, despite the obvious military requirement to ready his ship for battle that the situation generated.

The number of contacts grew from one to three as the distance between them closed. Soon, it was seen to be *Hornet* with two prizes: the salt-laden American merchant ship *William*, once prize to *Java*, and the British schooner *Eleanor* (or *Ellen*), which was carrying a cargo valued at $150,000. Lawrence had come out of port when *Java* and *William* first were sighted on 29 December, and had remained hovering off the entrance ever since, keeping *Bonne Citoyenne* covered and yet being in a position to evade should *Constitution* be defeated or additional enemy units appear. Bainbridge came to anchor offshore and *Hornet* ran alongside, her tops manned and the crew bellowing out three lusty cheers. Lawrence came aboard and updated the Commodore concerning events in the port, then the frigate got underway and entered Sao Salvador at 1 that afternoon. *Hornet* remained offshore to nab *Bonne Citoyenne* should the Briton choose to leave while *Constitution* was busy offloading prisoners and making repairs.

Prisoner offloading began at 2 P. M. on 2 January 1813. The Commodore had arranged a parole for all of them with General Hislop and Lieutenant Chads whereby they would return to England, not to fight in this war again prior to formal exchange. Among the last to leave was poor Captain Lambert, in dreadful pain from the musket ball that had broken a rib, punctured a lung, and come to rest near his spine. As he waited on a couch under an awning on the quarterdeck, a limping Bainbridge, suffering himself and supported by two of his officers, came to Lambert and returned his sword, saying, "I return your sword, my dear sir, with the sincere wish that you will recover, and wear it as you have hitherto done, with honour to yourself and your country." Lambert died on the evening of the 3rd, but this one act of Bainbridge's ameliorated any animosities existing between victors and vanquished and, in fact, General Hislop and the Commodore remained corresponding friends to the ends of their days. Lieutenant Chads, in his initial report of *Java*'s loss to the Admiralty, expressed his "grateful acknowledgements, this publically [sic], for the generous treatment Captain Lambert and his officers experienced from our gallant enemy, Commodore Bainbridge and his officers."

Bainbridge now had to consider his next course of action. There still was no sign of *Essex*. (She already was farther south at the rendezvous off Cabo Frio at this time.) *Constitution* had been mauled in the fight and really wasn't fit for extended cruising far from home. British forces in the area would be rallying to his presence soon, and would be bent on revenge. And there was *Bonne Citoyenne*. Weighing all these factors, the Commodore decided to head back home, taking with him *Hornet*'s two prizes. *Hornet*, he ordered to remain off Sao Salvador until *Bonne Citoyenne* sailed, or superior British forces appeared, or until about the 25th of January, when she was to head for home, reconnoitering Dutch Surinam and British Guiana along the way. All four ships departed Sao Salvador on the afternoon of January 5.

During this homeward trip, Bainbridge wrote his complete reports of the engagement and many letters to a circle of friends. One of these that has come down to us indicates that the Commodore was not a totally happy man. In a letter to John Bullus, then Naval Agent at New York, he made a much more open assessment of the damage his ship had suffered, and then made the surprising statement that, "...My Crew owing to the constant Exercise we give them, are very active & clever at their Guns. but in all other respects they are inferior to any Crew I ever had..." Was it the crew that had steered the wheelless ship and handled its sails in a brilliant maneuvering contest with a faster-sailing enemy that he was criticizing? Did he really mean it? Was he laying the groundwork for defending himself against criticisms of the casualties incurred or the damage received? Or unfavorable comparison with Hull's and Decatur's achievements? There seems to have been an abiding negative streak in Bainbridge.

When *Constitution* appeared off Boston Light on 15 February, the city had been aware of Bainbridge's victory for six days. First public notice of it had been given during a performance of "Hamlet" at the Boston Theatre. In the audience that night were Commodore John Rodgers, Captain Isaac Hull, and some other officers.

Adverse winds prevented the ship from entering the harbor immediately. When Bainbridge finally was able to come ashore at Long Wharf on the 18th, the city was ready for him. The route to the Exchange Coffee House was decorated with flags and streamers. A procession was formed at Faneuil Hall which included the Ancient and Honorable Artillery Company, the Boston Light Infantry, and the Wilson Blues. The tall Commodore was escorted by John Rodgers and the stumpy Hull, as well as other notables. Two bands played. And for the next two months Boston and the country gave themselves up to honoring the latest naval heroes. Congress again voted a gold medal to a skipper of *Constitution*, and silver medals for the junior officers, and also voted $50,000 in lieu of prize money to reward the *Constitution*s for *Java*. Bainbridge realized $7500 from this largesse; the average seaman or ship's boy received about $60.

The loss of *Java*, the third British frigate to be defeated in 4 1/2 months (Captain Stephen Decatur, in *Constitution*'s sister ship, *United States*, had beaten *HMS Macedonian* as Bainbridge was leaving Boston), led the Admiralty to take positive action. Gunnery training was revitalized. Small ships of the line were razeed (cut down) and larger frigates built to counter these American champions. And, effective immediately, no frigate of the Royal Navy was to engage an American 44 one-to-one; only when in squadron strength was the Royal Navy to take on an American heavy frigate. Thus, fifteen years after she was launched, *Constitution* had proved conclusively the correctness of her designer's work.

# NOTES:

1. Three eyewitnesses in *Constitution*, Surgeon Amos A. Evans, Midshipman Henry Gilliam, and Boatswain's Mate James Campbell, later wrote separately that the reason Bainbridge headed to seaward was because the contact was thought to be a 74, and that he doubled back when it became apparent that she really was a frigate. If true, it was a prudent course of action, but certainly not the stuff popular heroics are made of. Bainbridge, ever sensitive to his image, found "nobler" motives for the maneuver when the time came to write his report, stating that he hadn't wanted neutral territorial waters providing a safe haven for his opponent.

2. Marine Sergeant Adrian Peters, stationed in the main top, generally is credited with having felled the British Captain.

3. A moment of levity occurred during the first moments of post-battle elation when Lieutenant John T. Shubrick, in charge of the second division of 24-pounders, appeared topside with one coattail missing. In the heat of battle, it had gotten caught under the breech of a recoiling gun and he had cut it away with a jack knife. One observer though he looked like a plucked pigeon.

4. Because Bainbridge's battle bill is in the archives of the Naval Historical Center, it is possible to determine the distribution of American casualties in this engagement: four were wounded on the forecastle, and six killed and eight wounded on the quarter deck; below, there was one killed and four wounded each in First and Second Divisions, and two wounded in Third; aloft, one was killed and four wounded in the main top. Ironically, Daniel Hogan, the sailor who returned an ensign to the fore-mast in the midst of the *Guerriere* fight, had fingers shot off both hands on this occasion.

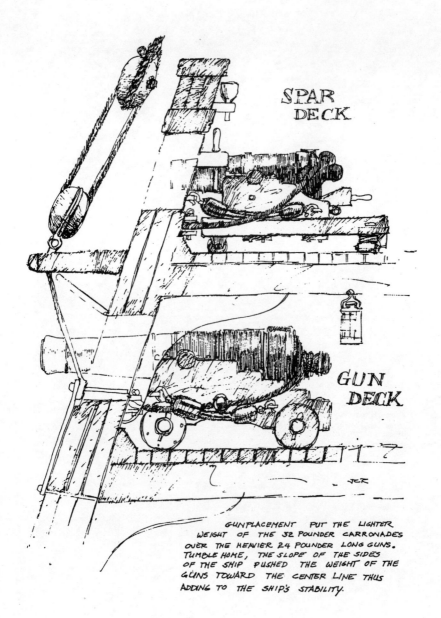

SPAR
DECK

GUN
DECK

GUNPLACEMENT PUT THE LIGHTER
WEIGHT OF THE 32 POUNDER CARRONADES
OVER THE HEAVIER 24 POUNDER LONG GUNS.
TUMBLE HOME, THE SLOPE OF THE SIDES
OF THE SHIP PUSHED THE WEIGHT OF THE
GUNS TOWARD THE CENTER LINE THUS
ADDING TO THE SHIP'S STABILITY.

# PART III

Commodore Bainbridge returned to Boston in mid-February 1813 and resumed command of the Navy Yard. And since *Constitution* was there undergoing battle damage repair, he retained command of her, too — until July, when Captain Charles Stewart arrived to prepare her for another war cruise.

Charles Stewart came of Irish stock, red-headed, and a couple of inches above average height. He was born in Philadelphia in 1778, the youngest of eight children of a merchant captain who died when Charles was two. His stepfather arranged a billet as cabin boy for him at the age of 13, when his limited formal education ended. Nearing his twentieth birthday, and already a qualified skipper, Stewart accepted a lieutenancy in the new Navy in March 1798. He served in *United States*, 44, and commanded *Enterprize*, 12, in the Quasi-War with France, and commanded *Siren*, 16, in the Barbary War, for which service he was awarded a sword by Congress. He achieved his captaincy in 1806, but, like Bainbridge, obtained leave to reenter the merchant service. Again like Bainbridge, he was back in Washington late in 1811 to pursue a combat command in the imminent war. In December 1812, he was given command of *Constellation*, 38, but she was blockaded in Norfolk, Virginia, before he could take her to sea. A sympathetic Navy Secretary (William Jones, Secretary since early in

1813) then ordered him to *Constitution* in Boston, where a British blockade had yet to be established so tightly.

Unfortunately for Stewart, the great need for seamen in the Great Lakes squadrons siphoned off all available manpower during the best months of the year, and he was unable to sail until late December. Once out, he headed into the Atlantic east of the Caribbean, then came west along the South American coast and into the Caribbean itself. He had some small successes and had departed for Bermudian waters and then on to the English Channel when he found his mainmast cracked and threatening collapse. The frustrated Stewart put into Boston for a replacement in April 1814 — and was immediately trapped by a greatly invigorated British blockade.

By mid-December, when bad weather played havoc with ships in coastal waters, the blockaders had been reduced to the frigates *Newcastle* and *Acasta*, and the brig-sloop *Arab*, 18. All of the others had been reassigned or were, as in the case of *Leander* at Halifax, in upkeep. Sunday, the 18th, dawned fair and clear, with a fresh breeze from the westnorthwest. To seaward, there was no enemy in sight. At 2 that afternoon, Stewart set sail and his longed-for moment was at hand. Cheered by people massed on Long Wharf and by the privateer *Prince De Neufchatel*, 18, "Old Ironsides" glided swiftly down the harbor and out to the open sea, the only American frigate running free. Wrote Chaplain A. Y. Humphreys in his journal:

> "We felt that the eyes of the country were upon us and that everything within the bounds of possibility was expected from us... [T]he fact was to present itself, that whatever might be our success there was little chance of being able to realize a safe arrival to port, should we be in anywise crippled by an equal force or by disaster of the ocean..."

Stewart looked for stragglers from the British blockading squadron off the Delaware and Chesapeake Bay and, finding none, headed for a position on the shipping lanes west of Bermuda. After taking one small merchantman prize, he headed farther southeast seeking the convoy from which she had straggled. He had no success in this endeavor and, nearing the Leeward Islands, turned back to the northeast, bound for the Bay of Biscay, and, he hoped, an eager British foe.

On 8 February, Stewart met and boarded a Hamburgh bark and later a Russian brig, both providing news that a peace treaty allegedly had been signed between Great Britain and the United States. Without official notice, however, Stewart was under orders to continue his cruise. Business as usual for him and, presumably, any Briton he met.

*Constitution* remained patrolling an area off Cape Finisterre, Spain, for the next several days, taking one British merchant ship prize. From her master, he learned that a British frigate said to be carrying millions in specie was due from South America, heading home. The Captain decided to head southwest and try and intercept her as she cleared the Atlantic narrows.

The 20th of February 1815 dawned cloudy and hazy with a cold, damp eastnortheast wind propelling *Constitution* in a southwesterly direction under short canvas, on a course roughly paralleling the African coast. Madeira was about 180 miles to the westsouthwest. All was quiet, but Stewart was keeping an alert watch because his activities of the preceding ten days certainly must have stirred up a hornet's nest off Gibraltar, a major Royal Navy base. At about 1 that afternoon, a ship was spied on the larboard bow, heading toward the American. In half an hour, a second contact was sighted beyond the first and somewhat to westward, "both standing close hauled towards us under a press of sail..." It was clear that the first unit was a full-rigged ship and probably a combatant. So matters stood until near 3 p.m., when the nearest contact signaled to the other and turned southward, apparently so the two could join company. Stewart instantly crowded on sail in pursuit, setting his stunsails as the big frigate gathered way. He was certain he had two Britons before him and thought their maneuvering meant they intended to keep away from him until nightfall when they could elude him. Every stitch of canvas was set in *Constitution*, alow and aloft. At about 3:45 p.m. a sickening cracking sound gave warning to those below that the main royal mast was giving way. Slowing his pursuit, Stewart quickly sent men aloft to cut away the wreckage while others prepared a spare spar. In an hour, it was aloft and the main royal drawing smartly once more. With the range closing again, *Constitution* "fired on the chase from the first gun 1st division and the chase gun on the forecastle..." The range was too great.

It was apparent that the enemy would be able to combine forces before Stewart could come up on the nearest ship, so he cleared for action and made deliberate preparations for battle. Shot was gotten up and powder charges made ready. The decks were sanded. Gun crews were divided to man the guns, port and starboard, simultaneously. Personal weapons for the boarders were broken out and positioned in tubs about the decks, ready at hand. And Surgeon John A. Kearney and his mates made their preparations down in the cockpit for the grim work they knew lay ahead of them.

About the time *Constitution* resumed the chase, the enemy "passed within hail of each other, shortened sail, hauled up their courses, and appeared to be making preparations to receive us." Stewart knew now he had his sought-after fight before him. After briefly trying to get the weather gauge and not succeeding, the Britons "formed on a line of wind at half a cables length from each other." (That is, they formed a column heading westward with the wind coming over their starboard quarters and with about one hundred yards between them.) The smaller of the two was in the lead.

A little after 5 p.m., *Constitution* broke the Stars and Stripes as she came ranging up on the windward side of the enemy column. They responded by hoisting Red Ensigns. At about 5:20 p.m., "Old Ironsides" was alongside the aftermost ship at about six hundred yards with her sails lifting gently, her momentum carrying her forward until she was in a position at the apex of an isosceles triangle, her opponents' column forming the baseline. From this ideal position, Stewart, standing near the larboard entry port for a better view, "invited the action by firing a shot between the two ships which immediately commenced with an exchange of broadsides." A British ball killed two men nearby in the waist and continued its way to smash one of the ship's boats. Firing continued hot and heavy for about fifteen or twenty minutes, when enemy fire slackened markedly, their shots falling short. By this time, the sea and the combatants were smothered in smoke, and the sun was lowering across the western horizon.[1] In the smoke and dimming light, the aftermost Briton altered course to starboard to close the distance and get his guns into more effective range. Stewart ordered a cease fire to allow the smoke time to drift clear ahead and to determine the condition of his opponents. It took a few minutes before the aftermost of his opponents came into view, and appeared to be luffing to cross under his stern and rake.[2] Blasting a final broadside into the smoke where he assumed the leading enemy

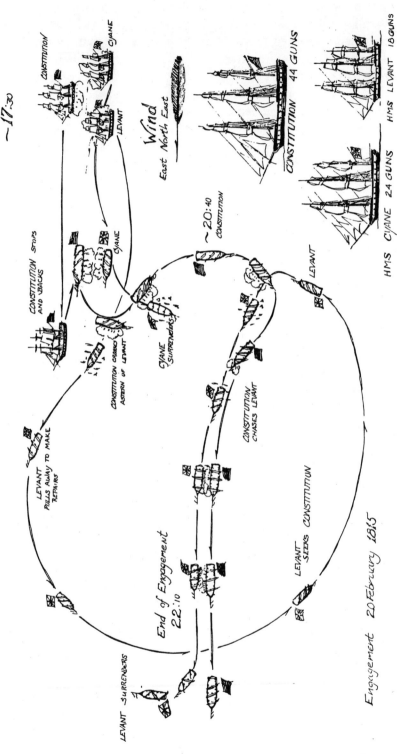

~ 17:30

CONSTITUTION
CYANE
LEVANT

Wind
East North East

CONSTITUTION 44 GUNS

HMS LEVANT 18 GUNS

HMS CYANE 24 GUNS

Jan Charles Roach
1992

CONSTITUTION STOPS AND BACKS

CYANE

CONSTITUTION CROSSED ASTERN OF LEVANT

CYANE SURRENDERS

~ 20:40
CONSTITUTION

LEVANT

CONSTITUTION CHASES LEVANT

LEVANT PULLS AWAY TO MAKE REPAIRS

LEVANT SEEKS CONSTITUTION

End of Engagement 22:10

LEVANT SURRENDERS

Engagement 20 February 1815

Sunset about 17:50 LZT

49

was, Stewart threw his main and mizzen topsails flat aback, with topgallants still set, shook all forward, let fly his jib sheet, backed swiftly astern, and unleashed a heavy fire. The rear enemy attempted unsuccessfully to wear away, receiving much damage to his sails and rigging, and a hail of musketry, in the process. He fell out of control, coming to his bow in a southeasterly direction, sails flat aback and headsails and spanker either ruined or snarled in wreckage. As this was happening, the leading enemy appeared out of the smoke, seemingly trying to get across *Constitution*'s bow and rake *her* from ahead; but Stewart once again filled his sails, boarded his foretack, and shot forward. When the enemy wore to larboard, Stewart rewarded him with two raking broadsides in the stern from a hundred yards, at which time the Briton ran off to leeward and darkness to escape the heavy fire and to restore order to gun crews that twice had attempted to desert their posts.

Looking east, Stewart saw that the larger of his opponents was attempting to get underway again. He wore short and slid into position on his larboard quarter. Just as he was about to give the starboard battery an opportunity from a range of just fifty yards, the enemy struck his colors, showed a single light, and fired a gun to leeward. The time was 6:45 p.m. In short order, Second Lieutenant Beekman V. Hoffman was aboard with fifteen Marines to take possession of *HMS Cyane*, 24, a light frigate under the command of Captain Gordon Thomas Falcon.

At 7:45 p.m., having taken the enemy officers into *Constitution* and assured himself that his prize crew could control *Cyane*, Stewart set off after the other enemy. That ship had not, in fact, run away, but had, instead, drawn off to affect repairs to her sails and rigging, and was returning to the fray. Thus it was that, within fifteen minutes of setting sail, Stewart found himself bearing down on an enemy which, in turn, was heading for him. At 8:40 p.m. the two passed each other at fifty yards going in opposite directions and exchanged starboard broadsides. The enemy then wore to run with the wind. Stewart adroitly wore short and got in a stern rake before he was out of range. Realizing how unequal the contest was, the latter made all sail, seeking escape. Stewart quickly was in chase, and at 9:30 p.m. began picking away at him with two bow guns, every shot being carefully sighted and few missing. The range steadily decreased until the American seamen could hear planking being ripped up as their shots told. Some of these sounds may have been those of the wheel, which was located abaft the mizzen mast, being shot away. Because his rudder tiller was positioned above the main deck, the enemy couldn't use stern chasers. A few minutes after 10 p.m., as *Constitution* was ranging up on the larboard quarter and recognizing there could be no escape, he came by the wind and also fired a leeward gun. Third Lieutenant William B. Shubrick went over to accept the surrender of HMS *Levant*, a new 18-gun corvette commanded by Captain George Douglas, the senior of the two British captains. A midshipman accompanying Shubrick has left this record of his first sight of *Levant*'s quarterdeck area:

> "The mizen [sic] mast for several feet was
> covered with brains and blood; teeth, pieces of bones,
> fingers and large pieces of flesh were picked up from
> off the deck. It was a long time before I could
> familiarize myself to these and is possible more
> horrid scenes that [sic] I had witnessed."

The British ships had sailed from Gibraltar on the 16th as units of a covering force spread out to protect convoys bound for England and the West Indies. After a brief stop at Tangiers for provisions, they had sailed "in trail" of the West Indies convoy with a mission of preventing it being surprised from astern. *Cyane*, the larger of *Constitution*'s opponents, carried thirty-four guns into this fight: twenty-two 32-pounder carronades, ten 18-pounder carronades, and two long 9-pounder chase guns. *Levant* carried eighteen 32-pounder carronades, one 12-pounder carronade, and, again, two long 9-pounder chase guns. Whatever their aggregate weight of metal, their strength lay in short range weapons whose maximum effective range was on the order of four hundred yards. In contrast, *Constitution* carried the batteries that had served her so well in this war: thirty long 24-pounders, twenty 32-pounder carronades, and two 24-pounder "shifting gunades".[3] The maximum effective range of her long guns was about twelve hundred yards - three times greater than that of the carronades - and gave Stewart the option of fighting at longer ranges when it was advantageous to do so.

The absence of records makes it difficult to assess crew sizes and casualties with precision. *Constitution* appears to have had 451 officers and men aboard at the time of the engagement, while, in round numbers, *Cyane* had 180 and *Levant*, 140. *Constitution*'s log states that she suffered four dead and fourteen wounded that evening, although most authors have stated three dead and twelve wounded (three mortally). A list of these crewmen, alluded to in Stewart's report, is missing. (It is known that none were officers.) As regards the British losses, estimates by Americans on the scene place the death toll in *Cyane* at twelve and in *Levant*, twenty-three; they counted twenty-six wounded in the former and sixteen in the latter. The bulk of these undoubtedly occurred as a result of the repeated rakes "Old Ironsides" poured into both ships; being a night action, Marine snipers only briefly made the sort of contribution they had in previous engagements.

British gunners in this fight appear to have concentrated more on the American frigate's hull than they had in previous encounters. Aside from a few lines cut in the opening blasts of grape shot, *Constitution* suffered only the loss of her foretopgallant yard aloft; her hull, on the other hand, was found to have about a dozen 32-pounder balls embedded in it - none of which opened a serious wound. *Constitution*'s heavy batteries, though, had wreaked havoc on her opponents. All of *Cyane*'s lower masts had been wounded, and the main and mizzen masts were tottering; every bowline and brace but one had been shot away; also wounded were her fore yard, main topgallant yard, gaff, driver boom, crossjack, fore topgallant mast, and fore and mizzen topmasts, the latter falling during this period. Five or six of her carronades had been dismounted as the lighter scantlings of her hull failed to stop the American's "heavy iron." She had been hit eight to ten times between wind and water. *Levant*, as has been noted, had her wheel shot away. Her rigging, too, had been decimated, all her lower masts were wounded and the mizzemast was threatening to fall, the main topgallant yard had been shot away,and the hull was pierced below the waterline by several shot.

In summary, Charles Stewart and *Constitution* had everything going for them in this fight: heavier gun batteries (although he could only suspect so beforehand); a tough hull better able to resist damage - with spars and rigging to match; and, thanks to the fact that the British blockade had put so many Americans on the beach, Stewart had been able to ship what was perhaps the most experienced crew "Old Ironsides" ever would have. Captain Stewart himself proved to be a superb tactician and shiphandler who took advantage of every break he got and acted decisively to deny the enemy any. He fought at ranges which ensured his gunners rarely would miss while his enemies were working beyond their maximum effective range. His experienced crew, in which he had the greatest confidence, was able to respond with alacrity to his demanding orders for swift and certain sail handling. If his adversaries can be said to have done anything "wrong," it would have to be having had the temerity to challenge him in the first place. On that day, in those circumstances, Stewart, *Constitution*, and the crew simply were unbeatable.

It required but three hours to put *Constitution* back in condition for further action, but the same could not be said of her prizes. The next day, Stewart was able to get the three underway on the southwesterly heading, moving slowly away from the major British naval base at Gibraltar while boats plied back and forth between captor and captives as American working parties sought to repair the results of their recent handiwork, and as prisoners, prize crews, and baggage were redistributed. Repairs were completed a week later, by which time Stewart had decided to head for the Cape Verde Islands, where he would parole the Britons and take on fresh stores before returning across the Atlantic.

*Constitution* and her prizes anchored in the harbor of Porto Praya at 11 a.m. on 10 March, after *Levant* narrowly had avoided running aground as they entered. Stewart was suspicious of Portuguese neutrality, but received assurances from the Governor on that score and a promise that the countryside would provide him with the fresh provisions he desired. He was able to make arrangements for his prisoners, as well.

The next morning, Stewart began shifting prisoners to a chartered British brig and had sent a working party of seventeen ashore to load stores. About noontime, Third Lieutenant Shubrick had just assumed the duty as Officer of the Deck when he was attracted by the stifled exclamation of a British midshipman and the apparent whispered reprimand he was receiving from his lieutenant. As he was trying to determine what had caused the little byplay, his quartermaster called his attention to the harbor entrance where a low, heavy fog covered the sea. Visible above it were the upper masts and sails of a ship. That must have been what had startled the midshipman. Captain Stewart was called immediately. By the time he reached the deck, two more sets of upper sails came into view, obviously the rigs of warships; all three were bound into the harbor. No doubt recalling that the American frigate *Essex* had been taken by the British in the neutral port of Valparaiso in 1814, Stewart took instant action to get his ships to sea, where he would have maneuvering room. Quickly, his crew was called to their stations. Just four minutes after sighting the last two contacts, he cut his anchor cable, set topsails, and stood out of the bay on a course calculated to give him the weather gauge for whatever was to follow. Signals to *Cyane* and *Levant* ordered them to follow suit, which they did with an alacrity that testifies to the competence of their prize masters and small crews.

*Constitution* and her consorts just cleared East Point, marking the northern limit of the harbor, as their pursuers came into long cannon range from the south. The enemy crowded on sail. What Charles Stewart did not learn until much later was that his pursuers were *Leander*, *Newcastle*, and *Acasta*, those three frigates especially built to counter "Old Ironsides" which had held her blockaded for eight long months in Boston. After learning of her escape, Commodore George Collier headed for the English Channel with this group. Failing to find his quarry there, he had patrolled southward until he received positive sighting information from one of the merchant ships *Constitution* also had boarded. After that, it became only a matter of time before the two sides would meet again.

The chase was continuing at a smart ten knots. It was observed that *Acasta* gradually was weathering on both *Cyane* and *Levant*, but not on *Constitution*, which slowly was pulling away from her consorts. At 1:10 p.m. Stewart signaled *Cyane* to tack to the northwest. This she did - without drawing a single enemy after her. The British Commodore evidently intended solely to "get *Constitution*." (*Cyane* got back to the U.S. safely, was purchased by the U. S. Navy for $40,000 in 1815, and served actively until 1827. She finally was broken up in 1836.)

At 2:30 p.m., one of the pursuers tried firing at *Constitution*, but the range was too great. By 3 p.m., it was becoming apparent that *Levant* was being endangered as *Cyane* had been. Hoping to divide the enemy and thereby improve the odds for them both, at 3:12 p.m. Stewart signaled to her to tack to the northwest. This time, all three pursuers tacked after the smaller vessel. *Constitution* quickly sailed over the horizon and out of danger. (The British trapped *Levant* in neutral verdict waters and forced her surrender.)

*Constitution* stood south until she reached the latitude of Guinea, then headed southwest in solitude, still hoping that the horizon ahead would be broken by the welcome appearance of the specie-bearing frigate. Cabo de Sao Roque, the northeast corner of Brazil, was sighted on 26 March. Stewart turned northwest. When, four days later, he received the morning report noting but 6000 gallons of "fresh" water remaining, he decided to put in at "Maranham" (Maranhao Island, the community was and is named Sao Luis), at the mouth of the Itapecuru` River.

Fourth Lieutenant William M. Hunter was sent ashore to make contact with local government officials and learn the latest news. He returned shortly saying it would be all right to land the prisoners and arrange for their return to England, but that no one yet knew whether peace had become a fact. The Americans were only too glad to be rid of their "passengers."

Stewart got underway for home on the 13th of April. *Constitution* arrived off San Juan, Puerto Rico, on the morning of 28 April, and Stewart sent Lieutenant Hunter ashore for the latest intelligence. Late that afternoon, he returned with confirmation that the peace treaty had been ratified. (In fact, America had ratified the Treaty of Ghent on 17 February, but because there was a 12-day "time late" clause built into it to provide time to communicate that fact to the farflung naval units on both sides, *Constitution*'s capture of *Cyane* and *Levant* stood as valid wartime conquests. The British recapture of *Levant*, however, technically was after the fact.)

Stewart took his departure from Puerto Rico late the next morning, bound for New York, where he arrived off the Battery on the afternoon of 15 May. He marked his return with a fifteen-gun salute and went ashore to the plaudits of his fellow countrymen, enjoying much the same reception as Hull and Bainbridge had received in Boston. Even as the festivities peaked, the *National Intelligencer* made a prophetic proposal:

> "Let us keep 'Old Iron Sides' at home. She has, literally, become a Nation's Ship, and should be preserved. Not as a 'sheer hulk, in ordinary' (for she is no ordinary vessel); but, in honorable pomp, as a glorious Monument of her own, and our other Naval Victories."

Congress could do no less than vote Stewart a gold medal for his classic action, making him the third successive skipper of "Old Ironsides" to be so recognized and his ship the only one that could boast of having had all her captains in that war decorated. Stewart and his crew also received prize money for *Susanna* as well as the value of *Cyane* and *Levant* (the sum for *Levant* coming from the Portuguese Government, which had so supinely allowed its neutrality to be violated at Porto Praya).[4]

Following the festivities in New York, Stewart returned *Constitution* to Boston at the end of the month, where crew was paid off and Stewart departed on furlough on 16 July. The ship remained "on call" until early in 1816, when she, too, was placed in reserve.

## NOTES:

1. Sunset occurred at 5:48 p.m.

2. The enemy actually was trying to close the range in any way possible before *Constitution*'s cannonade left her an unmanageable wreck.

3. The "gunades" had been among sixty-six captured by the Portsmouth, New Hampshire, privateer *Fox* in the British brig *Stranger* and sent safely into Salem, Massachusetts, in September 1814, from whence Captain Stewart acquired them, replacing four carronades on the spar deck. These guns, shorter than long guns (and 875 pounds lighter) but longer than carronades, had been designed by Sir William Congreve (he of rocket fame) and first produced in 1814. They were mounted on regular ship carriages like conventional long guns to permit ready shifting from one side of the ship to the other. Stewart had installed one on the forecastle and the other on the quarter deck.

4. Prize agent for *Constitution's* 1815 captures was John W. McCauley, Captain Stewart's brother-in-law.

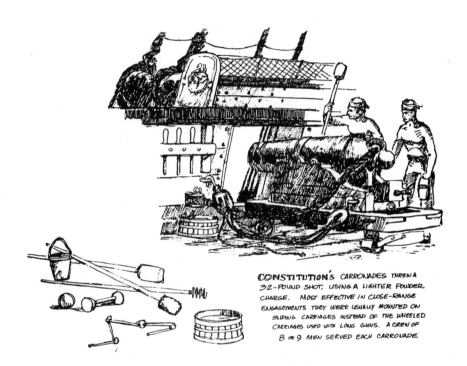

CONSTITUTION'S CARRONADES THREW A
32-POUND SHOT, USING A LIGHTER POWDER
CHARGE. MOST EFFECTIVE IN CLOSE-RANGE
ENGAGEMENTS THEY WERE USUALLY MOUNTED ON
SLIDING CARRIAGES INSTEAD OF THE WHEELED
CARRIAGES USED WITH LONG GUNS. A CREW OF
8 OR 9 MEN SERVED EACH CARRONADE.

# AFTERWORD

Objective analysis of the War of 1812 must conclude that the victories of *Constitution* and *United States*, together with those of *Essex* and the war-brigs, had no direct effect on the course of the war. The losses suffered by the Royal Navy were no more than pin pricks to that great fleet: they neither impaired its battle readiness nor disrupted the blockade of American ports. By comparison, Oliver Hazard Perry's fresh-water victory on Lake Erie in 1813 and Thomas Macdonough's on Lake Champlain a year later prevented the overland invasion of the United States and determined the course of the war.

What *Constitution* and her sister did accomplish was to uplift American morale spectacularly and, in the process, end forever the myth that the Royal Navy was invincible. They demonstrated unmistakably that the American man-of-warsman was every bit as good as his British cousin and that his ship could stand with the best. The big frigates made Americans proud to be Americans, proven equals to any other nation in the world. They won the second War for Independence.

As we now know, *Constitution*'s days of daring battles and stirring victories were at an end. She and her men had accomplished far more than any single ship in our naval history. However, as we also know, she still had duties to perform -- and many miles to sail under the Stars and Stripes.

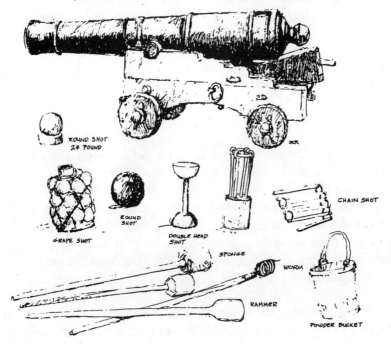

WEIGHT, ABOUT 6,500 POUNDS
POWDER CHARGE, 8 LBS.
MAXIMUM RANGE, ABOUT 1,500 YARDS
(ACCURATE TO 300-400 YARDS)

AMERICAN 24-POUNDER GUN

ROUND SHOT
24 POUND

GRAPE SHOT

ROUND
SHOT

DOUBLE HEAD
SHOT

CHAIN SHOT

SPONGE

WORM

RAMMER

POWDER BUCKET

60

# APPENDIX A

## *CONSTITUTION*'S CASUALTIES IN VICTORY OVER *HMS GUERRIERE*

### 19 AUGUST 1812

#### Killed

1LT William S. Bush, USMC[1]          Quarterdeck

Seaman James Ashford

Seaman Robert Brice[2]

Seaman John Brown

Seaman James Reed

Seaman Jacob Sago

Seaman Caleb Smith

#### Wounded

Lieutenant Charles Morris[3]          Quarterdeck

Sailing Master John Aylwin[4]          Quarterdeck

Seaman William Dunn[5]

Seaman Daniel Lewis          #15 Long Gun

Seaman George Reynolds          1st Loader, #5 Carronade

Seaman Owen Taylor

Private Francis Mullen[6]

*Notes:* 1. Shot through head.

2. Lost his life "through want of precaution in not sponging His Gun being blown from the Muzzle of the piece."

3. Shot through abdomen.

4. Shot in right shoulder.

5. Lost a leg; pensioned.

6. Shot in the ankle while serving in Mizzen Top.

# APPENDIX B

## *CONSTITUTION*'S CASUALTIES IN VICTORY OVER *HMS JAVA*

### 29 DECEMBER 1812

### Killed

| | |
|---|---|
| Seaman Joseph Adams | #10 Carronade |
| Seaman John Cheevers[1] | 2d Sponger, #9 Long Gun |
| Seaman Patrick Conner | #8 Carronade |
| Seaman Barney Hart | 2d Loader, #11 Carronade |
| Seaman Jonas Ongrain | 3d Loader, #5 Long Gun |
| Seaman Mark Snow | Helmsman |
| Ordinary Seaman John D. Allen | Helmsman |
| Ordinary Seaman William Cooper | 1st Sponger, #9 Carronade |
| Private Thomas Hanson | Main Top |

### Wounded

| | |
|---|---|
| Captain William Bainbridge[2] | Quarterdeck |

| | |
|---|---|
| Midshipman Lewis Germane | #9 Long Gun |
| Master's Mate Charles Waldo[4] | Main Top |
| Quartermaster Peter Woodbury | Leading Helmsman |
| Seaman Enos Bateman | 1st Loader, #4 Carronade |
| Seaman Philip Brimblecomb[4] | 1st Loader, #1 Long Gun |
| Seaman Joseph P. Cheevers[1,4,5] | 2d Loader, #5 Long Gun |
| Seaman John Clements[8] | Main Top |
| Seaman Philip Cook | 2d Captain, #5 Carronade |
| Seaman Abijah Eddy | 2d Sponger, #9 Carronade |
| Seaman Peter Furnace[6] | Powder Monkey, #12 Gun |
| Seaman James D. Hammond | 2d Sponger, #10 Carronade |
| Seaman William Long | 1st Captain, #5 Long Gun |
| Seaman Reuben Sanderline[5] | T. Tackle, #11 Carronade |
| Seaman Stephen Sheppard | 3d Sponger, #9 Long Gun |
| Seaman Joseph Ward[7] | T. Tackle, #5 Carronade |
| Seaman Stephen Webb[5] | Captain, #4 Carronade |
| Seaman William Weeden | 1st Loader, #12 Long Gun |
| Seaman Nicholas Wextram[9] | 2d Loader, #4 Carronade |
| Ordinary Seaman Samuel Brown | 2d Sponger, #5 Carronade |
| Ordinary Seaman Daniel Hogan[10] | Fireman, #9 Long Gun |
| Ordinary Seaman John Vogel | Shotman, #5 Long Gun |

| | |
|---|---|
| Ordinary Seaman John Vogel | Shotman, #5 Long Gun |
| Ordinary Seaman Thomas Williams[11] | 1st Sponger, #9 Long Gun |
| Private Michael Chesley | Main Top |
| Private John Elwell | Main Top |
| Private Anthony Reeves | ? ? ? |

*Notes:* 1. Brothers.

2. Wounded twice, the first a fragment of copper rod in the quadriceps a few inches above the knee, and the second, contusions from several splinters.

3. Died of a grapeshot wound which damaged a clavical and scapula, and caused internal bleeding.

4. Lost an arm.

5. Died of his wounds.

6. Died of complications from being hit by a grapeshot in the lower leg which lodged in the achilles tendon.

7. Lost a leg.

8. Leg shot off above the ankle; due to severe lacerations, amputated just below the knee.

9. Also listed as Vixtram.

10. Had fingers on both hands shot away.

11. Third man of this name in crew.

# APPENDIX C

## *CONSTITUTION*'S CASUALTIES IN VICTORIES OVER *HMS CYANE* AND *HMS LEVANT*

### 20 FEBRUARY 1815

**Killed**

Seaman Thomas Fessenden

Seaman John Fullington

Private Antonio Farrow

Private William Horrell

**Wounded**

14 enlisted men, including

Seaman Tobias Fernald[1]

Private John Lancey[2]


Notes: 1. Arm amputated. Died 12 Mar 1815.

2. Wounded in both thighs; one "shattered." Died 22 Feb 1815.

# BIBLIOGRAPHY

Abbreviations used in this bibliography:

| | |
|---|---|
| ADM | Admiralty |
| CAPT | Captain |
| CDR | Commander |
| CHAP | Chaplain |
| COMO | Commodore |
| LCDR | Lieutenant Commander |
| LT | Lieutenant |
| MHS | Massachusetts Historical Society |
| MIDN | Midshipman |
| NA | National Archives |
| NHC | Naval Historical Center |
| PRO | Public Records Office |
| RG | Record Group |
| RN | Royal Navy |
| SURG | Surgeon |
| USMC | United States Marine Corps |
| USN | United States Navy |
| 2LT | Second Lieutenant |

## MANUSCRIPT SOURCES:

Bryon, Thomas C. Narrative of the Cruises of the U. S. Frigate *Constitution*. 1861 Ms. Private collection.

Clear, Sailing Master Michael, USN. Affadavit. 25 Nov 1825. NHC.

Court Martial Record, LT Henry Ducie Chads, RN, 23 Apr 1813. PRO (ADM 1/5435).

_____, CAPT James R. Dacres, RN, 2 Oct 1812. PRO (ADM 1/5431).

_____, CAPT Lord George Douglas, RN, 1815. PRO (ADM1/5449).

_____, CAPT George Thomas Falcon, RN, 1815. PRO (ADM1/5449).

General Order, CAPT Charles Stewart to crew, 23 Feb 1815. RG45, NA.

Journals, MIDN Frederick Baury, 24 Jun-26 Oct 1812 and 28 Oct 1812- 16 Feb 1813. MHS.

Journal, SURG Amos A. Evans, 11 Jun 1812-15 Feb 1813. Private Collection.

Letter, COMO William Bainbridge to Sailing Master Bill, 23 Jan 1813. NHC.

Letter, COMO William Bainbridge to Dr. John Bullus, 23 Jan 1813. Maine Historical Society.

Letter, COMO William Bainbridge to William Jones, 5 Oct 1812. Historical Society of Pennsylvania.

Letter, CAPT William Bainbridge to COMO John Rodgers, 13 Sep 1812. RG45, NA.

Letters, COMO William Bainbridge to SecNav, 2 and 13 Sep, and 24 Oct 1812, and 13 Apr 1813. RG45, NA.

Letter, 2LT John Contee, USMC, to Lewis Bush, 13 Sep 1812. Private collection.

Humphreys, CHAP Asheton Y., USN. "Recapitulatory Journal." Ms. Lilly Library, Indiana University.

Letters, MIDN Henry Gilliam to CAPT William Jones, 7 Sep 1812 and 16 Feb 1813. Georgia Historical Society.

Letter, Charles W. Goldsborough to SecNav, 7 Oct 1818. RG45, NA.

Letter, CAPT Isaac Hull to COMO John Rodgers, 2 Sep 1812. RG45, NA.

Letter, CAPT Isaac Hull to SecNav, 1 Sep 1812. RG45, NA.

Letter, CAPT Isaac Hull to Benjamin Silliman, 29 Oct 1821. Yale University.

Letters, SecNav to CAPT William Bainbridge, 9 Sep and 2 Oct 1812. RG45, NA.

_____, SecNav to Navy Agent George Harrison, 10 and 16 Sep 1812. RG45, NA.

_____, SecNav to CAPT Charles Stewart, 18 and 23 May 1815. RG45, NA.

Letter, CAPT Charles Stewart to SecNav, 2 May 1815. RG45, NA.

Letter, U. S. Naval Observatory to author, 1 Apr 1993.

Log, *USS Constitution*, 1-29 Aug 1812. Huntington Library.

Logs, *USS Constitution*, 1 Feb-13 Dec 1812 and 18 Dec 1814-16 May 1815. NA.

Muster Rolls, *USS Constitution*. NA

## PRINTED DOCUMENTS:

Boston (MA) Records, Vol. XXXVIII, p. 113.
U. S. Congress. *Annals of the Congress of the United States.* 12th
Congress, Second Session.

## MEMOIRS AND MONOGRAPHS:

Bailey, Isaac. *American Naval Biographer.* Providence:
author. 1815.

Campbell, James. *Glorious Naval Victory.* Broadside poem.
Boston. Ca. 1813.

Claxton, Lt C., RN. *The Naval Monitor.* 2nd. ed. London:
A. J. Valpi. 1833.

Cole, Alfred W., and Noble, Roderick, eds. "Our Portrait
Gallery (No. IX): The Hon. Justice Cloete, LL. D." *The
Cape Monthly Magazine,* Vol. VI, No. 84 (Oct 1859).

Cooper, James Fenimore. *Naval History.* Mason, Parker, &
Pratt. Ca. 1866.

Forester, C. S. *The Age of Fighting Sail.* Garden City:
Doubleday and Co. 1956.

Frost, LCDR Holloway H., USN. *We Build A Navy.*
Annapolis: U. S. Naval Institute. 1940.

Frost, John. *The Pictorial Book of the Commodores.* New
York: Nafis and Cornish. 1845.

Grant, Bruce. *Isaac Hull: Captain of "Old Ironsides."*
Chicago: Pellegrini and Cudahy. 1947.

Hollis, Ira N. *The Frigate Constitution.* Boston:
Houghton, Mifflin and Co. 1901.

James, William. *Naval Occurrences.* London: T. Egerton.
1817.

_____. *The Naval History of Great Britain.*
London: Baldwin, Craddock, and Joy. 1824.

Maclay, Edwin S. *History of the Navy.* 2 vols. New York:
D. Appleton and Co. 1895.

Mahan, CAPT Alfred T., USN. *Sea Power in its Relation to
the War of 1812.* Boston: Little, Brown and Co. 1905.

Maloney, Linda M. *The Captain from Connecticut: The Life
and Naval Times of Isaac Hull.* Boston: Northeastern
University Press. 1986.

Martin, CDR Tyrone G. USN (Ret). *A Most Fortunate Ship.*
  Chester, CT: Globe Pequot Press. 1980. Reprinted Norwalk,
  CT: Eaton Press. 1990.

Morris, COMO Charles, USN. *Autobiography.* Annapolis: U.S.
  Naval Institute. 1881.

Paullin, Charles Oscar. *Commodore John Rodgers.* Annapolis:
  U. S. Naval Institute. 1967.

Porter, COMO David, USN. *Journal of a Cruise.* Annapolis:
  Naval Institute Press. 1986.

Pratt, Fletcher. *Preble's Boys.* New York: William Sloane Assoc.
  1950.

Price, Norma Adams, ed. *Letters from Old Ironsides, 1813-1815.*
  Tempe, AZ: Beverly-Marion Press. 1984.

Roosevelt, Theodore. *The Naval War of 1812.* 3rd. ed. New York:
  G. P. Putnam's Sons. n. d.

Smith, Moses. *Naval Scenes in the Last War.* Boston: Gleason's
  Publishing Hall. 1846.

Thomas, R. *The Glory of America.* New York: Ezra Strong.
  1834.

Turner, Lynn W. "The Last War Cruise of Old Ironsides."
  *American Heritage*, Apr 1955.

## ARTICLES:

Adams, Charles F. "Wednesday, August 19, 1812, 6:30 P.M.:
  The Birth of a World Power." *American Historical Review,*
  18 (Apr 1913).

Martin, CDR Tyrone G. USN (Ret). "Isaac Hull's Victory
  Revisited." *The American Neptune,* Winter 1987.

Mould, Daphne D. C. Pouchin. "What It Was Like To Be Shot
  Up By 'Old Ironsides'." *American Heritage,* Apr/May 1983.

*National Intelligencer,* 23 May 1815.

## UNPUBLISHED MATERIALS:

Long, David F. "Bainbridge and His Navy." Ms. 1978.
  Published as *Ready to Hazard.* Hanover, NH: University
  Press of New England. 1981.

Martin, CDR Tyrone G., USN (Ret). "A Most Fortunate
  Ship." Revised and expanded ms. 1995.